Natural Disasters

erica rivera

ISBN-13: 978-1518604867
ISBN-10: 1518604862

For more by Erica Rivera, visit: www.ericarivera.net

DEDICATIONS

To the one I let go of.

To the one I long for.

CONTENTS

I'm bad weather and good sex,
Or vice versa.

~ Sherman Alexie

UNAVAILABLE

You call commuting
between Brooklyn
and Manhattan.
Pretend
you want to talk about
the weather.

Oppressive East Coast heat,
steam-spewing sewer grates,
the way you sweat through
your suit
on the subway.
"Get on a plane, baby.
Peel me free."

She can't even fathom
your heap of dirty laundry.
(Love is not blind.
It's naïve.)

But ours is a distance
that won't be traversed
with air travel.

Fight or flight,
our story
always ends
the same way.

"I need to see those
milky breasts, those
moony eyes."

You're wrong
(as usual).

My heart is the moon.
My eyes are the stars.

And you, bittersweet,
are the sun.

We coincide,
sometimes,
but cannot co-exist.

One of us
must
say   goodbye.

MUDDY WATERS

Mist rises in foggy swirls over the water
I start off early
Slowly stroke the lake with my paddle
Ripples chase my worn canoe
But never seem to catch up
Pine and warm cinnamon scents
Remind me of an uncommon life
On this majestic and ever-changing patch of Earth
When I was young I lay on these shores
Fingertips creating gentle tessellations in the moisture
Distorted reflection dissecting every movement
Childhood lost is found again as my boat
Drifts under a willow tree
The vines licking my cheeks
Soft as a mother's touch
My canoe comes to a sauntering halt
Feet rebel from shoes
Coolness tickles my toes
Submerged in a collage of seaweed and sand
I fabricate fables for each cloud
As night falls
Graceful loons dance across the water
Sound out
Tear at my eardrums
I hear chants from a campfire several docks away
I see the blistering flames climb and fall
I smell burnt marshmallows
Intoxicated

BEFORE THE BRUISES

There were breezes brimming with salt
and cigarette smoke
you in your cowboy hat
bearded, anhedonic

I in the butterfly freckled blouse
hiding a strap
that kept coming unclasped

Your fingers fixin' to be inside
settled for tongue
in front of everyone

Before the bruises
there were breakfast breads
and roadside phone calls
coy questions and
bonfire flirtation

We were a mismatch
made for disaster
but went ahead breakneck
because…why not?

This is how I choose
to remember you:
slender and clean
as an unlicked reed

Wild
beyond the constraints
of your skin

GIGAWABAMIN MENAWAH

I wouldn't mind being anesthetized
until I see your face next time.

Quiet so I can keep you,
half-asleep these weeks in-between.

My brain an incubator
of tête-à-tête we haven't had yet.

Desire, a feral dog,
gnashes its fangs, paces,

desperate to escape
domestication.

Lucky you, who fucks and runs
(or rather, flies) away.

I don't fault you for your freedom but I want
to tag along. Unaccompanied, you

return to the land of
palm trees and two seasons,

return to the land of
screen-printed sunsets,

return to the land of
undergrads, tan legs perpetually spread.

I stay and sink further into the muck
politely referred to as my life,

practicing Ojibwe and waiting for the day
I can spell your name

across your bare back,
b-e-l-o-v-e-d.

HEIRLOOM

This love is a shovel
Eden waits beneath our feet

    Dirt, the purest form of prayer
    painted on naked knees

        The hard-earned tartness of harvest
        drips from your chin

            Welcome to the first bite
            of the rest of your life

FOURTH OF JULY

We melted together

    like Neapolitan, two scoops

        on a humid afternoon

        like fireworks

            across a movie-screen sky

WORDS CAUGHT CROSSWAYS
IN A WOMAN'S THROAT

The first night we collided
a twister ripped through town.
The rest of the world witnessed
wind-wrecked trees,
hail-ravaged roads,
an apocalyptic skyline.
I didn't see a thing.
I was cocooned
in the ecstatic cyclone
of your arms.

ATMOSPHERIC PRESSURE

I drive west
into the fierce inferno sunset.

The holiday
weekend weather

as absurd as
our affair.

By the time I arrive
clouds fade to black.

White diamonds flutter
onto eyelashes.

"It's snowing!"
you say.

And for a moment
delight

in something less
predictable than us.

UNTITLED FOR L

I.

His couch hijacked your stuff.

That's how this all started.

A sacral chakra rock
once relied upon for luck
is gone.

It must have served its purpose
if it led you to his lair
where
the furnace whispers
as your breath harmonizes
with his heart

beat.

Just before he
fell asleep
he stroked his hairy chest
and teased,
"You stole my chi."

Now his growly sounds
thrum
through the room.

Your body tender,
sticky and sour.
This
is worth the risk
of almost anything.

II.

You leave.

Reluctantly?

Yours is the only car
that drives at this hour
yet the sky is
bright and alive.

You write at red lights,
grappling for the fastest pen,
fingers flipping through Post-it
notes.

When the lines
won't be restrained
you know you're a goner.

III.

Home.

Alone.

You undress to find
you're holding his sock
hostage
by mistake.

Decide to keep
one piece
of evidence
just in case.

Silent and surrendered
remembering his fist resting
on your chest
as he slept.

But what you wanted most
in the months before him
was not sex
per se

but the kind of laughter that
rattles your belly
renders you breathless
and blushing.

Independence? Overrated.
You can do everything on your own
except incite
that level of silliness.

IV.

A man who didn't want you
once declared,
"You are demanding fire."

Swore another would stay
despite the writing.

What if
this is him
and instead
you
are the one
afraid?

V.

And if he never asks you
a question to say yes to?
He'll live on in this poem.
No.
This is not a poem
(you don't know how to write those)
but a tired attempt at making sense
of that which has no words.

ACROSS A CROWDED THEATER

how strange to see you
upright and finely clothed

your arm around another
in public, lover

to clamor from afar
for those wicked lips

to be cursed with thirst
for your attention

tragicomedy
this dénouement

now she reads
from the script I wrote

the one where we end up
enamored

WAKE UP

How can you sleep through
autumn sunrises? Don't you
know beauty beckons?

GOING, GOING, GONE

These boots await a
reason to leave like black cats
looking for trouble.

MATE FOR LIFE

Afternoon. Two ducks
fucking, emotion-free and
crude. I thought of you.

KOAN

Why are the leaves on
the tops of the trees always
the last to fall off?

KISSING AT THE AIRPORT

I forget this isn't illicit.

You sling an inked arm
around my shoulder
at MSP.
Your kiss, unsolicited,
lands on the edge of my lips.

I forget this isn't illicit.

You left LAX with baggage.
(A metaphor, maybe,
given the chaos of your latest
uncoupling.)
It went to DEN.
Delayed indeterminately.
(Definitely a metaphor.)

I forget this isn't illicit.

Though we share beds with lists of lovers,
arrivals, departures,
here, we're
free to choose each other.

I forget this isn't illicit.

Shotgun,
you search for vacancies.
Antsy, eager teenagers, we.
"Motel 6?"
"My standards are low, but hell no."

I forget this isn't illicit.

Damien Jurado has a song called
What Were The Chances.

Let's make it ours.
"It's not like we're cheating.
We're only meeting
in hotels and not your home."
I play it on repeat when I'm without you.

I forget this isn't illicit.

We agree one key will suffice.
The proprietor inquires:
"You won't be fighting tonight?"
"No fighting," you confirm.
No sleeping over, either.
In so many ways, we're not intimate at all.

I forget this isn't illicit.

We intertwine every month or two,
catch up, sprawled, in numbered rooms.
You stretch possessively across
my collarbones, cupped hands holding
my seams together,
wet mouth ending the drought.

I forget this isn't illicit.

My palm roams your prickly head.
I trace the outline of your eagle tattoo.
(Why is he so angry? I wonder.)
Hypnotized by your impossibly
smooth skin, I breathe:

"I forget this isn't illicit."

"Isn't it?" you ask,
voice buffered by a pillow.
(Legally, we're still married to other people.)
If I reveal what's hidden within—
that I would sacrifice an empire to lie
by your side every night—
will you concede

this isn't illicit?

FIFTY BAGS AND COUNTING

Why
Do we do this
Every autumn
Buy bags made from trees
To trap jewel-hued leaves
Then sell them back
To the garbage man
As compost
When will we see
Nature can't be contained
When will we listen
To what she needs

BELATED

Every year, I forget my father's birthday.
(September, I'm sure, though the date proves elusive.)
It passes by unrecognized.

Every year, my father reassures
his absentminded offspring,
"It's okay. We're all a little amnesiac."

Every year, the only one who calls him
is my mother, from whom
he's been divorced two decades.

11:11

When I see your face
in forty years I hope it's
smiling just like this

USE IT OR LOSE IT

Our hearts are muscles.
They remember how to love
when our brains do not.

AS AUTUMN WOULD HAVE IT

Eighty degrees. October.
Bewildered geese
invert their V over and over.

At least these winged things try.

You
remain unmoved
season after season.

BEAT THE CLOCK

Your watch
is my worst enemy.

A tick-tick-ticking
grenade

set to destroy
this pilfered time.

I want to smash
that stupid shiny circle

trying to confine us
in a clock-watching world.

Put that black-eyed
bomb away

and focus on my face
for once.

DAYLIGHT SAVING

I don't want
an extra hour

that slow
sickly shadow

fall back
into what?

it won't catch me
when I cave

the only thing
behind me is

sixty minutes more to
waste

as you have
half a century
today

DO NOT DISTURB

There's no fulfillment in this.

First-name-only envelopes.
Canary-eating grins.

Key card-operated elevators and
discreet bellhops who knowingly nod.

Rented, rumpled beds.
Mirrored walls. Bleach stench.

When you leave,
I am exquisitely

open
but empty.

RE: [NO SUBJECT]

Why is it so hard
to say
"I'm sorry"?

Those three syllables
would erase
everything that aches.

Words can be weapons, yes,
but better ammunition
is their absence.

FULL DISCLOSURE

You say you have to tell me the truth

As though honesty were optional

As though there were any other way to relate

A GIRL'S ALLOWED TO CHANGE HER MIND

November
Season of violet sunsets
And skin-shearing wind

In the car we sit
Stalemate
I say "no" and "stop" and "don't"
But you go
On and on and on

About how
One kiss
Would be sufficient
To see if the spark ignites

A Weeble-fat man in an orange hat
Watches from his snowless yard
As we rehash this toxic repertoire

Talking touching finger-fucking
Your tongue Tennessee Hot
(So much for that platonic lunch)
Invited inside, I'm inclined to oblige

When I exit, hours later
Mussed, discombobulated,
The orange-hat man remains,
Observes my walk of shame

Drama-mongering Minneapolis,
Smothered
By a wet duvet
Of white

IT HAPPENED TONIGHT

I opened my eyes. You, silhouetted in yellow light. Glistening tangles of
ginger hair. Pelvis pumping to primal rhythms. Face pinched tight.

Your mind was adrift
but imagining us.

Enjoying you enjoying me, the way you give and rescind until spilt.
Such relief. As if you've expelled something heavy.

Or found a part of
yourself gone lost.

LAYAWAY

You love me like
a battered leather jacket

for the familiar way
I drape across your back

for how easily
I can be left behind

A FRIENDLY REMINDER

the next time you want
to hurt me hit me instead
it will heal faster

HE SAID, SHE SAID

I could have sworn there was a map.
~ Peter Sacks

Winter

frozen smoke stack smog   to the gorge and back
slithers across the Mississippi skyline   on a tank of gas
this far north   I drive so fast
amidst dismal weather   the road becomes the Rio Grande
even pollution is pretty   and the cherry-red Astro, my raft

Spring

crabapple buds explode   the sky blackened, burst
like popcorn kernels on tree limbs   overnight
raincoat weather requires coffee   Taos turned green
I'm cold—and over-caffeinated   and the hills exhaled

Summer

in downward-facing dog today   my limbs now know New Mexico
I discovered   runner's feet slap cobblestone
a woven maze   that ancient Pueblo aroma
where spiders scurried   inescapable as smoke

Fall

lake now naked   cottonwoods shed
leaves unhinged   like serpent skin
the Buddhists say,   the sun so white
"Let go or be dragged."   I confuse it for the moon

End-of-Year Almanac

When I wax poetic about   a one-night stand so delicious
the weather what I mean to say is   I demanded seconds
I yearn for your clay-colored eyes   the way you played

34

the glistening globe of your head
I should have studied
the geography of your body
as closely as I did the land

my bones like piano keys
your caresses as
magnanimous
as the mountains

TRIAGE

cauterize my wounds
with your kisses
bury the scars
beneath my skin
only to resurface
when you gift them again

UNDERAPPRECIATED TWEETS

1. Sometimes I tell you yesterday's truths.

2. You can be offended or you can be amused.

3. Beware of men with big promises.

4. Nothing you could say would satisfy me. Satisfaction is in the action.

5. I'd rather be chased than be chaste.

6. Whoever wants it less has the most power, but whoever wants it more will find another way to get it.

7. Just because I give it away for free doesn't mean you don't have to earn it.

8. It feels so good to you because I care. Imagine how it feels to me, given that you don't.

9. Your heart is wrapped in barbed wire and I've no flesh to spare.

10. This is not love-making. This is animals attacking.

11. You're my blood sport, lover, and I, a sore loser.

12. Stop fighting *with* me and start fighting *for* me.

13. My name is not Jameson. My body is not your bar. Seek oblivion elsewhere.

14. You've ceased to amaze (much less surprise) me.

15. It's like you don't even care that I gave up on you.

16. Of all the things you've stolen from me, it's sleep I miss the most.

17. Your ghost is here, chastising me silently.

18.   I want to tell everyone about you but you're the only one I tell my stories to.

A COMMON LANGUAGE

The first phrase I learned
in your mother tongue was:
Ojiimishin![1]

Followed by:
Gego zhaagwenimoken![2]

And then:
Michaa![3]

In reference to:
Inde'.[4]

I will not look up:
I love you.[5]

Nor will I learn:
It's over.[6]

---

[1] Kiss me!

[2] Don't hold back! (Don't be shy!)

[3] It's big!

[4] My heart.

[5] I want to hear you say it first.

[6] What goes unspoken never ends.

THE MOURNING AFTER

Fragments of our conversation
come back to me
clear
as shattered glass.

If I could shake
my pen awake
would a poem
with your name interred
tumble out?

If I refuse to beg,
will you read
between
the lines of my
trembling lips?

LEFT UNSAID

Your idiolect has become
so ingrained on my tongue
that sometimes your words
masquerade as my own

You hold a grudge like flesh in a fist
an unforgiving grip on my throat
auctioning off the next breath
when all I want to relay is:

Remember when it started
December, Downtown
the corner where you kissed me
is now a crime scene

HOW TO SURVIVE JANUARY IN MINNESOTA

1. Read all the books written by Philip Roth. Twice.

2. Bake every recipe in the *The Pie and Pastry Bible* and eat results directly from the pan with a spoon.

3. Invite your ex over for a "nap," then steal his body heat.

4. Binge-watch all six seasons of *Sex and the City*. Re-enact the scenes between Carrie and Big with your bestie.

5. Open a Twitter account for a fictitious woman who drinks hard, sleeps around, and speaks her mind. Name her @misfitmpls.

6. Bundle up and waddle around the block.

7. Soak in a bubble bath until your toes prune. Drain water; repeat.

8. Shop for sexy funeral garb. Wait for your adversaries to die.

9. Create an online dating profile and specify "Men without hot tubs need not apply."

10. Write bad poetry. Self-publish it.

WELL ENOUGH

Well Enough
  doesn't like to be left alone

Well Enough
  wants to drag eyeliner across her lids
  prance around in precarious heels and pleather leggings
  karaoke *Doll Parts* poorly
  wreak havoc in alleyways

Well Enough
  won't be alone for long

CLASSICAL CONDITIONING

Do you believe,
as I do,
that most of life
is lived
out of habit?

If that's true,
then you,
like any vice,
can be unlearned.

THE WINTER OF OUR DISCONTENT

Are you a blessing or a test?
Am I the secret turned regret?

You bring the winter with you.
I am the warmth.
It's no match for your frostbitten heart.

Nothing ends; it ebbs.
With one exception:

ice.

POST-MORTEM

there are so many ways
a spirit can break
the morning after, you marvel
how the world goes on, unperturbed
tiger lilies flit on the vine
rocks remain steady in their neat little line

moribund no longer
slip on your gloves
and gardening clogs
dig up the dirt and cover the corpse
the earth will conduct
its own autopsy

peace, once so abhorred,
returns like robin song in spring
purged, you are pure
ripe and ready
for some new happiness
to bloom

REPEAT AFTER ME

Some men are uninhabitable.
Some missteps are unforgivable.

Either way,
the answer is the same:

Move on.
Move on.
Move on.

APRIL, FOOLS

Now that I've obliterated us,
don't you want to know when?

Saturday afternoon.
The W.

As you ate scrambled eggs, cross-legged,
Powell's etched across your pecs.

I sat opposite, blood-stained
sheets tucked under arms.

The modesty was false
but the falling was true.

I swallowed the sin of loving you.
I've heard what happens to women who do.

Only fools.

NO APOLOGIES

I dreamt of another man last night.
He burrowed his face
in my feverish breasts
and said:
"How could anyone rival
a heartbeat like that?"

ON SUNDAYS

we drive south
dirt road rising
in tires' wake, gaze
at how amber grains
really do wave
or how trees shake, irate
and the wind will whistle
if you listen long enough
the countryside conveys
more than humans ever could

MY FAVORITE PHOTOGRAPH

I have never seen such a smile
grace my father's face.

Cake cone in hand, ice cream almost gone.
Across his lips a slippery sheen of butter pecan.

His beard pristine as if debris
were swept away by a delicate hand.

Carrot hair, newly shorn.
The same shade I bore when I was born.

That smile on my father's face,
awestruck and adored.

YOU DON'T SAY

nonconsensual
silence is the only way
to get through to you

UNSENT TEXT

my hips
are homesick
for yours

UNFORGOTTEN

I reach across the mystery of you with words, write
a phosphorescent spotlight to tempt you towards the page
you were never mine but our memory is
and I cling to it

harder than the whiskey that sours you from inside out
harder than the gaggle of pretty girls that giggle at your wit
harder than your bloody steaks business deals bank accounts
harder than you hate your mean-fisted father

Maybe I didn't truly know you but I knew what I wanted to
that was enough, Irish eyes, and in the end
we all wish for our secrets, told
this is mine: I miss you still, and will, 'til every tomorrow dies

ABOUT THE AUTHOR

Erica Rivera's previous books include *Insatiable: a young mother's struggle with anorexia* (Penguin Group, 2009), *Man Eater* (XOXO, 2011), and *Come Again* (Thought Catalog Books, 2015). She is a prolific freelance writer, an award-winning poet, and a lifelong Minnesotan. *Natural Disasters* is her first published collection of poetry.

For more by Erica Rivera, visit: www.ericarivera.net

.

59327049R00038

Made in the USA
Charleston, SC
01 August 2016